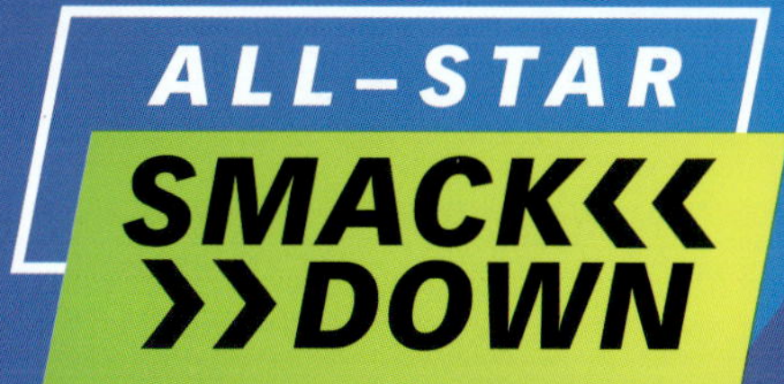

KYLIAN MBAPPÉ VS. THIERRY HENRY

WHO WOULD WIN?

PETER DOUGLAS

Lerner Publications ◆ Minneapolis

The stats and information in this book are accurate through April 2025.

Lerner Publications Company
An imprint of Lerner Publishing Group, Inc.
241 First Avenue North
Minneapolis, MN 55401 USA

For reading levels and more information, look up this title at www.lernerbooks.com.

Main body text set in Aptifer Sans LT Pro.
Typeface provided by Linotype AG.

Library of Congress Cataloging-in-Publication Data

Names: Douglas, Peter author
Title: Kylian Mbappé vs. Thierry Henry : who would win? / Peter Douglas.
Other titles: Kylian Mbappé versus Thierry Henry
Description: Minneapolis, MN : Lerner Publications, [2026] | Series: All-star smackdown (Lerner sports) | Includes bibliographical references and index. | Audience: Ages 7–11 | Audience: Grades 2–3 | Summary: "Kylian Mbappé and Thierry Henry are both all-time great soccer players. But which one is the best? Readers discover key stats, awesome highlights, and incredible wins and decide for themselves who comes out on top"—Provided by publisher.
Identifiers: LCCN 2025013689 (print) | LCCN 2025013690 (ebook) | ISBN 9798765689479 library binding | ISBN 9798348028411 paperback | ISBN 9798765694428 epub
Subjects: LCSH: Mbappé, Kylian, 1998-—Juvenile literature | Henry, Thierry, 1977-—Juvenile literature | Soccer players—France—Biography—Juvenile literature | Soccer players—Rating of—France—Juvenile literature | AS Monaco—History—Juvenile literature | Soccer—France—Juvenile literature | LCGFT: Biographies
Classification: LCC GV942.7.A1 D68 2026 (print) | LCC GV942.7.A1 (ebook) | DDC 796.334092/2—dc23/eng/20250521

LC record available at https://lccn.loc.gov/2025013689
LC ebook record available at https://lccn.loc.gov/2025013690

Manufactured in the United States of America
1 - CG - 12/15/25

TABLE OF CONTENTS

Introduction
Soccer Legends 4

Chapter 1
Journey to Success 8

Chapter 2
Great Moments 14

Chapter 3
Super Strikers 20

Chapter 4
And the Winner Is 24

Smackdown Breakdown. 28
Glossary. 30
Learn More 31
Index 32

Thierry Henry

INTRODUCTION

SOCCER LEGENDS

During a 2000 match against rivals Manchester United, Arsenal forward Thierry Henry took a pass with his back to the goal. Henry quickly flicked the ball up to knee height. Then he spun

FAST FACTS

- Thierry Henry played 123 matches for the French National Team and scored 51 goals.
- Henry played in four World Cup tournaments.
- Kylian Mbappé won the Golden Boot as the tournament's leading scorer after he scored eight goals at the 2022 World Cup.
- Mbappé is Paris Saint-Germain's (PSG) all-time-leading scorer. He has scored 256 goals in 308 appearances for the team.

and kicked a right-footed volley. The ball sailed 60 feet (18.3 m) into the net for a brilliant goal. Arsenal won the match.

Eighteen years later, Kylian Mbappé was only nineteen and playing in his first World Cup tournament for France. The French national football team is called *Les Bleus* because of their shirt color. *Les bleus* means "the blues" in French.

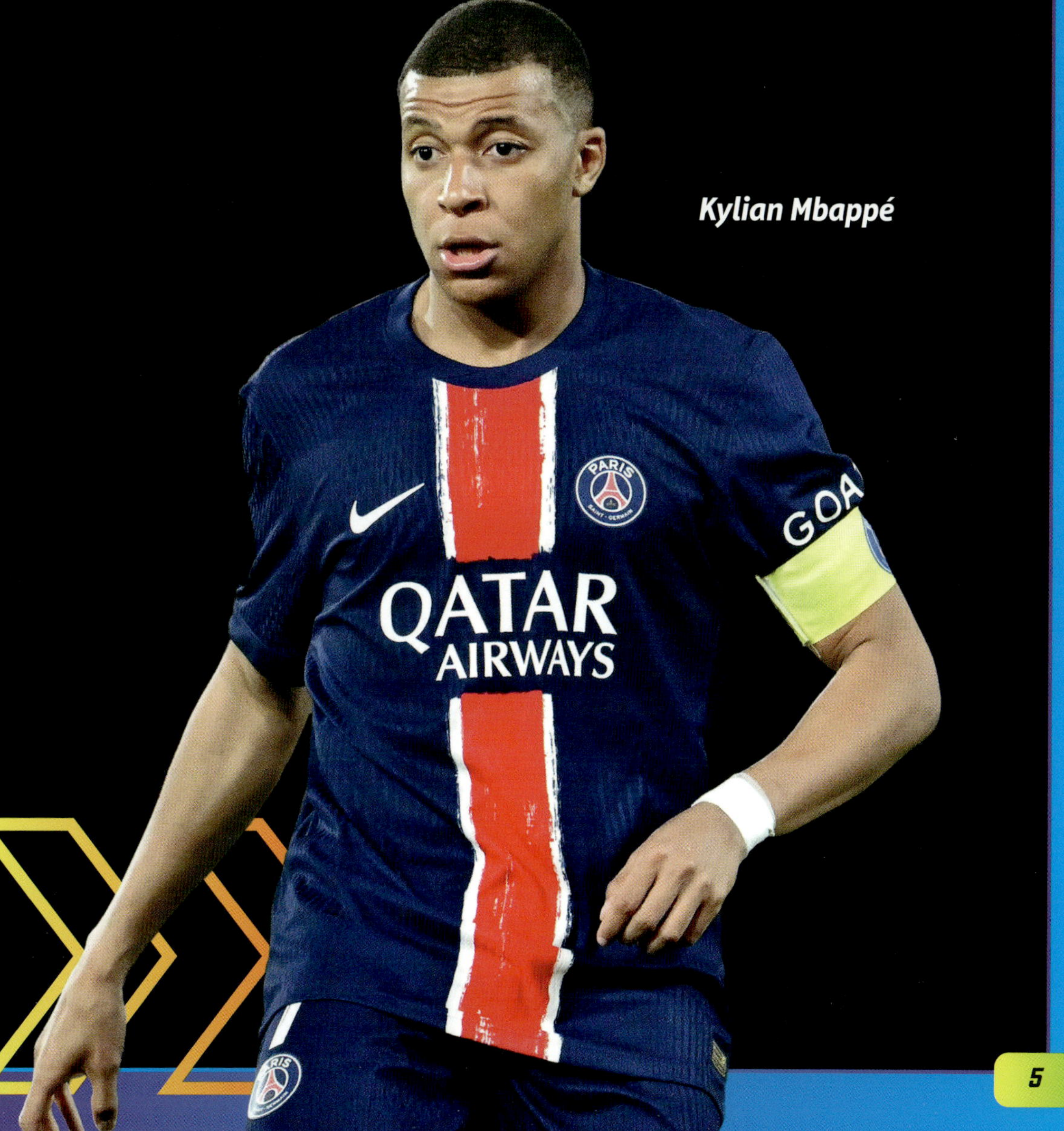

Kylian Mbappé

It was 34 minutes into France's second group stage match against Peru, and neither team had scored. French player Paul Pogba stole the ball from one of Peru's players. He passed the ball to Olivier Giroud, who fired off a quick shot.

The shot bounced off a defender, flew over the Peru goalie's head, and landed at Mbappé's feet. He streaked to the net and scored the only goal of the game. This goal made Mbappé the youngest goal scorer in World Cup history.

Henry and Mbappé are both superstar forwards. But who is the best? Let the smackdown begin!

Thierry Henry played for five different club teams during his pro career.

Mbappé celebrates a goal during a 2024 match against Poland.

CHAPTER 1

Henry avoids a defender while playing for AS Monaco during the 1998–1999 season.

JOURNEY TO SUCCESS

Association Sportive de Monaco (AS Monaco) is one of the most successful club teams in France. Thierry Henry and Kylian Mbappé are two of the best players in the club's history.

Thierry Henry was born in Paris in 1977. His skills were strong from a young age. A top-level youth soccer team recruited him when he was seven. AS Monaco scouts began taking an interest in him at age 13.

At around age 15, Henry joined the AS Monaco youth program. When he was 17, Henry moved up to AS Monaco's second team. A second team is often used as a practice squad, and players often serve as substitutes for the first team. Sometimes they play other clubs' second teams.

Opposing teams feared Henry's powerful right foot. He scored 175 goals in the English Premier League.

Henry played most of that season at this level, as well as eight matches with the club's top team. He made his pro debut on August 31, 1994.

The team's manager was Arsène Wenger. He noticed Henry's talent. Wenger left Monaco after the 1994 season. But he did not forget about Henry.

In 1997, Henry led AS Monaco to the league championship, the sixth in club history. In 1999, he left Monaco to play for Arsène Wenger at English Premier League (EPL) powerhouse Arsenal FC.

Henry celebrates a goal during a match between Arsenal and Aston Villa on October 16, 2004.

Kylian Mbappé celebrates after scoring a goal during a 2017 Champions League match against Manchester United.

Kylian Mbappé was born in Paris in 1998. Mbappé's father was a soccer coach who trained Mbappé from a young age. Many top club teams were interested in him, including Real Madrid, Manchester City, and Bayern Munich. Mbappé stayed close to home until June 2013 when he signed with AS Monaco.

Mbappé quickly moved up through the club's ranks. On December 2, 2015, at the age of 16, he played in his first pro match for AS Monaco's top team. In 2017, he led the team to the league title, the eighth in AS Monaco history.

Mbappé scored 175 goals in 205 games with PSG.

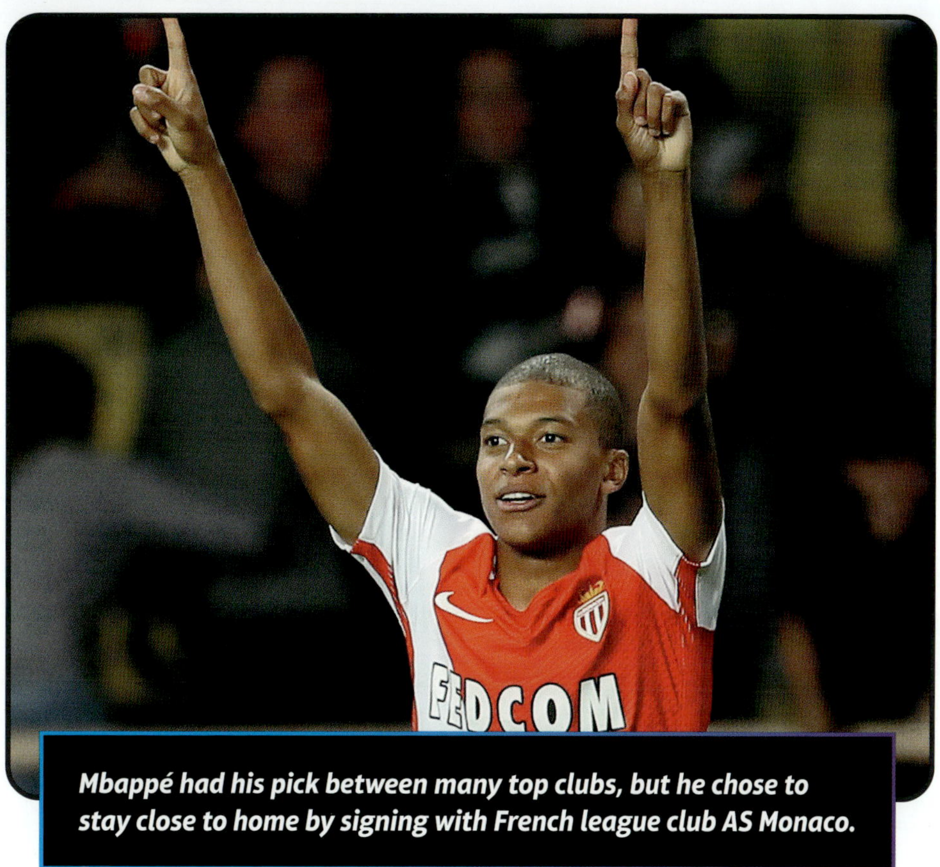

Mbappé had his pick between many top clubs, but he chose to stay close to home by signing with French league club AS Monaco.

After the 2017–2018 season, Mbappé left AS Monaco for his home team. He joined PSG and played there until 2024.

CONSIDER THIS

Monaco is an independent country, but it has no pro league. That's why AS Monaco plays in France's pro league. The club was founded on August 24, 1924.

CHAPTER 2

Henry (left) and Arsenal teammate Dennis Bergkamp won two EPL championships together, in 2002 and 2004.

GREAT MOMENTS

Many consider Thierry Henry's time at Arsenal to be the greatest EPL career of all time. He led the league in goals scored a record four times. Henry also helped Arsenal win two Premier League titles in 2001–2002 and 2003–2004.

In 2003–2004, Arsenal was undefeated. Henry was a big part of the team's success. He scored a league-leading 30 goals. One exciting goal came in a match against Liverpool. Early in the second half, the score was tied 2–2. Arsenal fans were worried their winning streak was about to end.

But then, Henry got the ball high in the Liverpool end. He dribbled straight at the Liverpool defense. He went around two defenders and booted the ball into the net. Arsenal took the lead. Henry scored again later in the match for a hat trick, and Arsenal kept their streak alive.

Henry left Arsenal in 2007 to play for FC Barcelona in Spain. Barcelona's top rival is Real Madrid. Games between the two teams are called *El Clásico*, which means "The Classic."

Henry during a 2007 match against the Glasgow Rangers.

Henry kicks the ball past Real Madrid keeper Iker Casillas in a 2009 El Clásico. Barcelona won the match 6–2.

Henry's most memorable El Clásico performance was on May 2, 2009. Henry scored to tie the game 1–1 in the 18th minute. Barcelona added two more first half goals to put them ahead 3–1 at the start of the second.

Real Madrid scored first in the second half, but before Real Madrid could think about making a comeback, Henry scored again. That goal wasn't just the game winner. It also stopped Real Madrid in their tracks. Barcelona went on to score two more goals for a 6–2 win.

Kylian Mbappé has also had many great moments in his young career. Some of his best moments were during his time with PSG.

CONSIDER THIS

In 2024, Henry said his season-saving goal against Liverpool was the most iconic of his career. He chose his run through the defense to score the game winner over seven of his other goals.

The UEFA Champions League is a European club tournament. The top club teams play throughout the season to determine the winner. In February 2021, PSG faced Lionel Messi and Barcelona midway through the tournament.

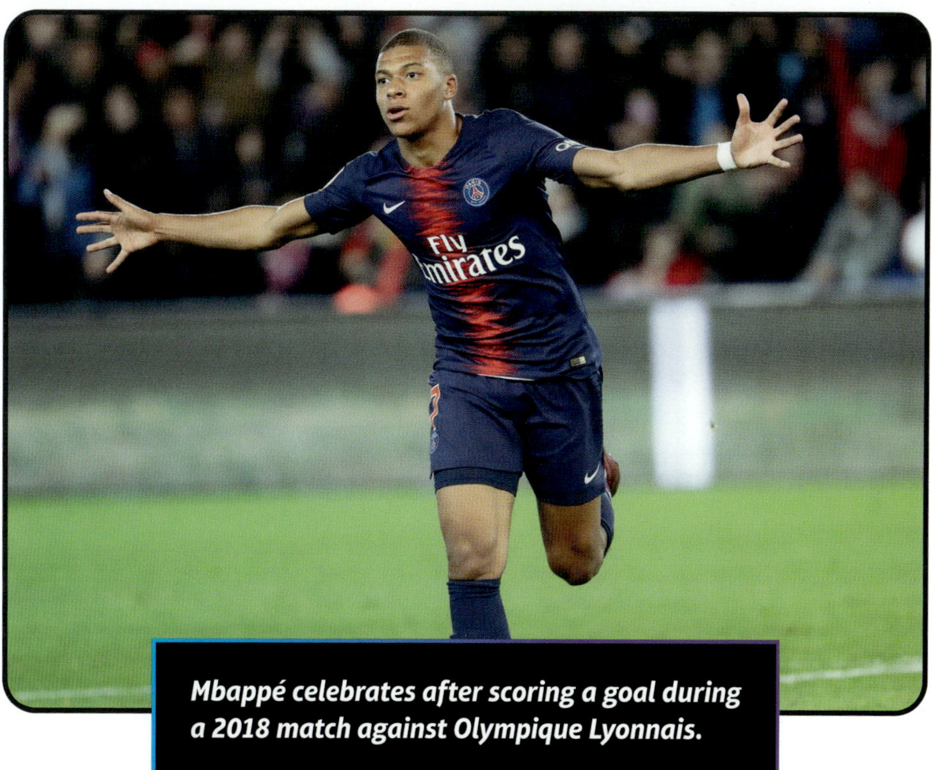

Mbappé celebrates after scoring a goal during a 2018 match against Olympique Lyonnais.

At only 22 years old, Mbappé had already played in two World Cup Finals.

Mbappé was amazing in the match. Messi scored first on a penalty kick. That's when Mbappé took over. He scored a goal in the first half to tie the game 1–1. Then, 20 minutes into the second half, Mbappé struck again for the game winner. PSG would add two more goals. One of those was Mbappé's third goal of the game, earning him a hat trick.

Mbappé's club career is one for the record books, but his biggest impact may be on the French National Team. In 2022, France was the defending World Cup champion. Mbappé did everything he could to help them win again. France advanced to the final where they faced Argentina. Argentina's captain was Mbappé's new PSG teammate, Lionel Messi.

Argentina jumped out to a 2–0 lead. Mbappé had to dig deep to give his team a chance. He scored two second-half goals to do just that. The match went to extra time. Argentina scored first. Once again, it was Mbappé who was the hero. He completed a hat trick by scoring on a penalty kick to tie the game with just two minutes remaining.

France went on to lose the match in a penalty shootout. But Mbappé had just made history. He was the second player in history to score a hat trick in a World Cup Final.

Mbappé celebrates after scoring France's first goal during the 2022 World Cup Final.

CHAPTER 3

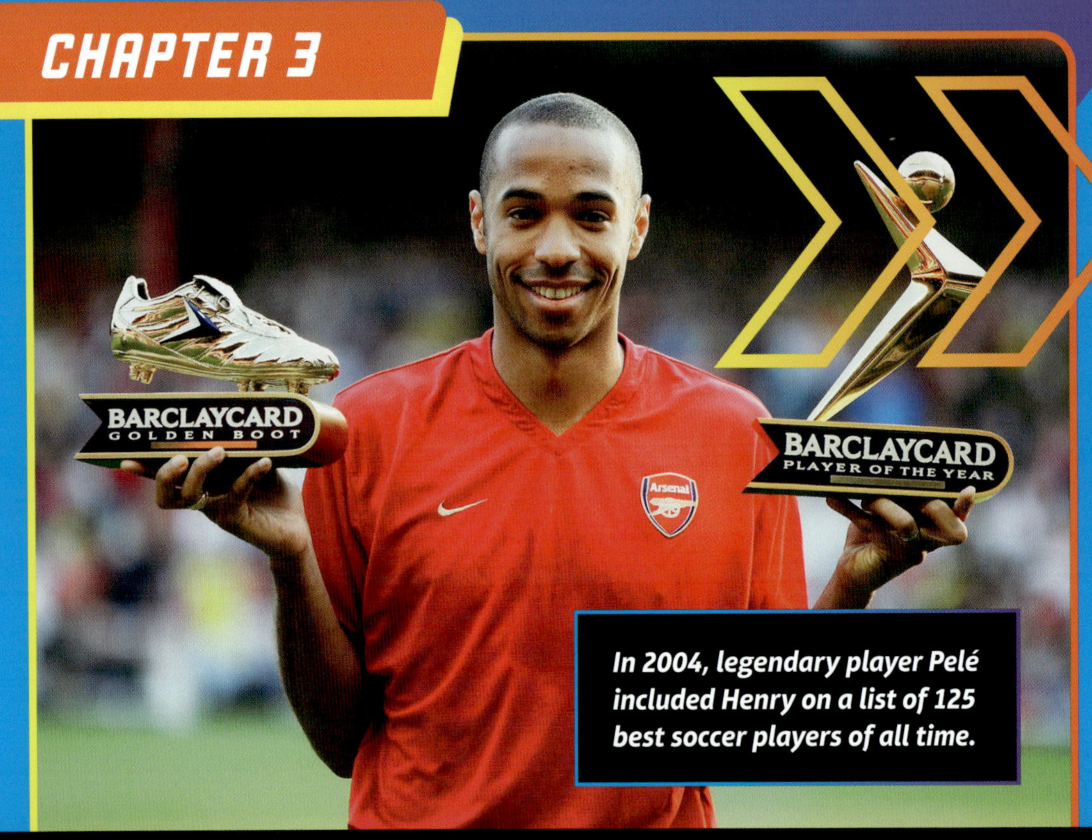

In 2004, legendary player Pelé included Henry on a list of 125 best soccer players of all time.

SUPER STRIKERS

Thierry Henry and Kylian Mbappé are not only two of the greatest French players of all time. Many would say they are also among the greatest players ever to play the game. Both men have played in two World Cup Finals. Each has won a World Cup trophy.

Thierry Henry set the EPL record for assists in a season with 20 in 2002–2003. He was voted Footballer of the Year in England that season. Henry won this award three times during his career. He was also named French Player of the Year five times. Mbappé has been named French Player of the Year five times so far.

Both players have set many records. Henry is Arsenal's all-time leading goal scorer with 175. He won five league championships and one FIFA Club World Cup. Henry also won the European Golden Boot three seasons in a row after leading Europe in goals in 2003–2004, 2004–2005, and 2005–2006. He is a two-time EPL Player of the Season, winning in 2004 and 2006.

After his playing career ended, Henry became a sports announcer on TV and later a coach.

Mbappé won the Best Player award in Ligue 1 in 2024.

Mbappé is PSG's all-time leading goal scorer. He scored goal number 201 in 2023 to break the club record. He scored a total of 256 goals for PSG.

Mbappé has helped his club teams win seven league titles. He led the French league in goal scoring five times. He also

CONSIDER THIS

Kylian Mbappé has played in two FIFA World Cups, making it to the Final both times. He scored four total goals in those finals. That's more than anyone else has ever scored in World Cup Finals games.

won a record five French league Player of the Year awards in a row.

At the 2022 World Cup, Mbappé scored eight goals to win the Golden Boot as the leading goal scorer in the tournament. In 2024, he was also the leading scorer in the UEFA Champions League competition. Mbappé scored eight goals in that tournament. This helped PSG make a run to the semifinals, where they eventually lost to Borussia Dortmund.

Mbappé celebrates after winning the 2018 FIFA World Cup.

CHAPTER 4

Mbappé became the captain of Les Bleus in 2023. He scored two goals in his first game as captain.

AND THE WINNER IS

This is a close matchup. Thierry Henry has an edge because of his long career. He was one of the world's best players for 10 years. But Mbappé is only 26 and has many years left to play. At this same stage in his career, Henry had about half as many goals and about half as many assists as Mbappé. A lot will depend on the rest of Mbappé's career.

Mbappé has the talent to dominate at Real Madrid just as Henry did at Arsenal. He also has the opportunity to do more on the international stage as France's team captain. If his future is anything like his past, Mbappé is likely to pass Henry in every area.

Henry served as Arsenal's captain during his last two seasons with the club.

In the end, the winner of this smackdown is Mbappé by a thin margin. The world will have to watch as he continues to build his legacy to see if it can stack up to Henry. Mbappé certainly has the time and the skill to do it.

Which player do you think is the best? Will it be the legendary striker or the rising star with a world of potential? Consider their strengths and decide for yourself!

Henry brings the ball up the field during a 2009 match.

Mbappé celebrates after defeating FC Barcelona in 2024.

SMACKDOWN BREAKDOWN

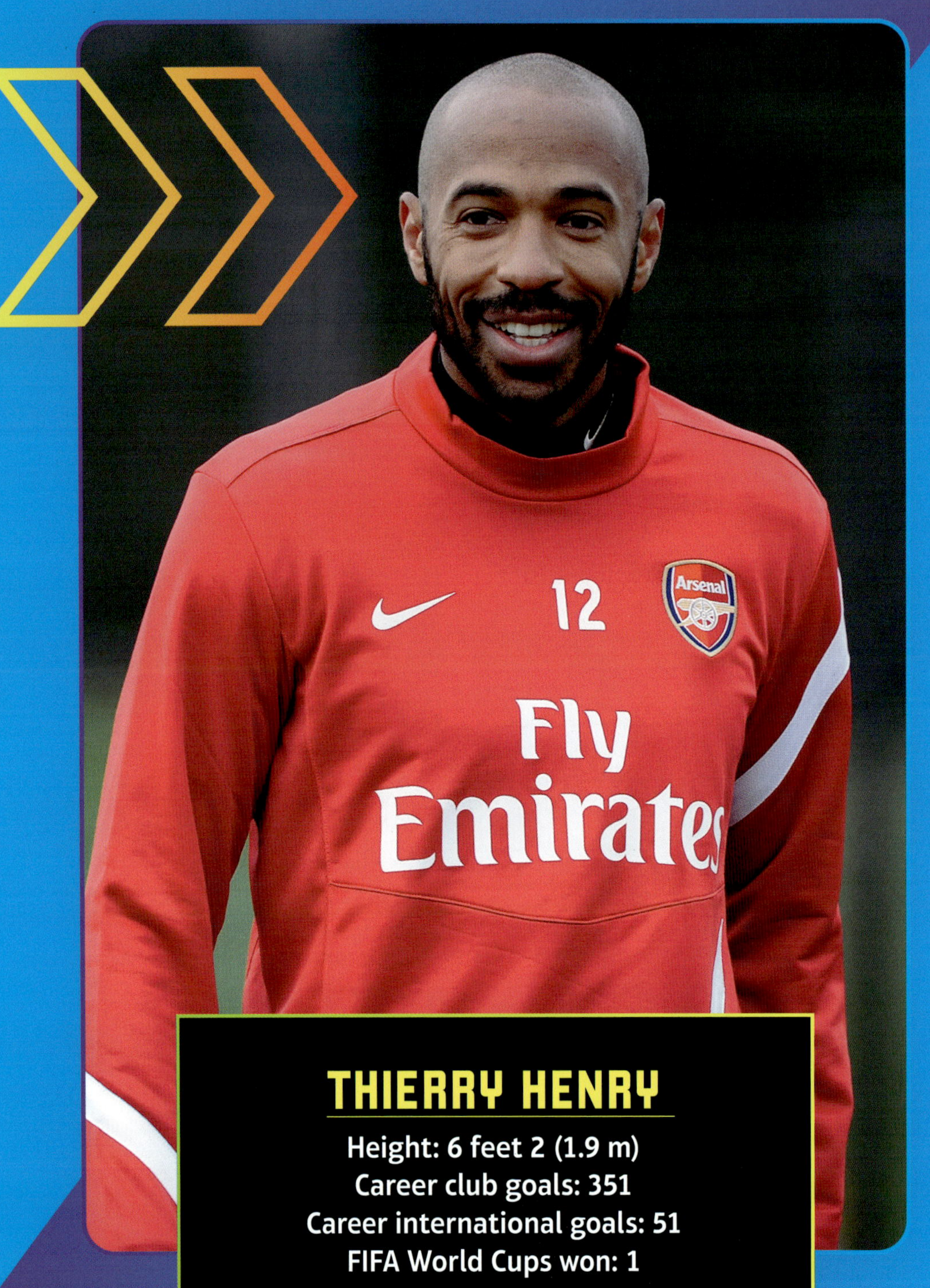

THIERRY HENRY

Height: 6 feet 2 (1.9 m)
Career club goals: 351
Career international goals: 51
FIFA World Cups won: 1

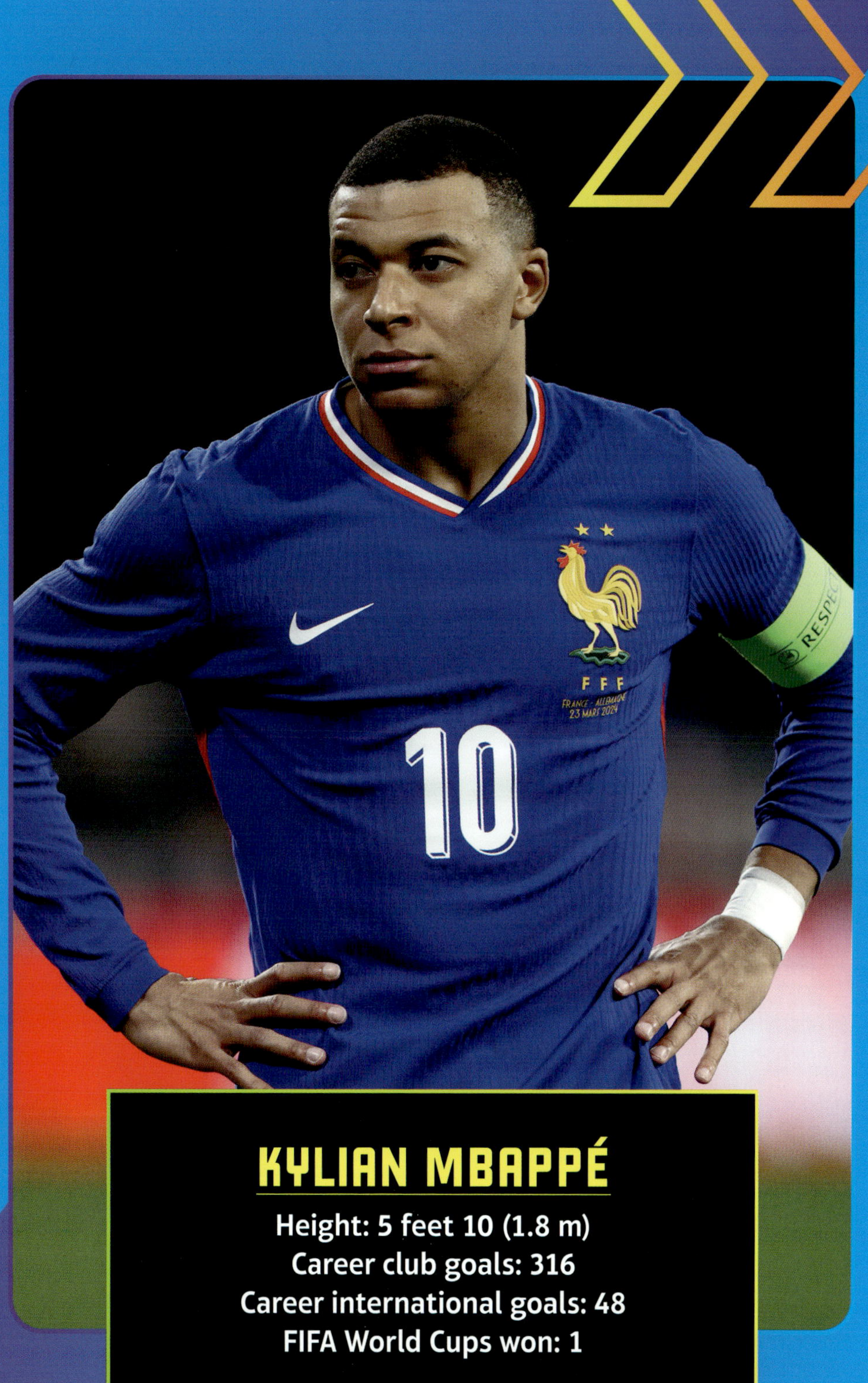

KYLIAN MBAPPÉ

Height: 5 feet 10 (1.8 m)
Career club goals: 316
Career international goals: 48
FIFA World Cups won: 1

GLOSSARY

assist: a pass from a teammate that leads directly to a goal

club: a pro soccer team

dribble: to move and control the soccer ball with the feet

forward: a player whose main job is scoring goals

group stage: the first round of a tournament

hat trick: when a player scores three goals in a game

penalty kick: a free kick at the goal following a foul

tournament: a series of contests played to determine a champion

volley: to kick the ball before it touches the ground

LEARN MORE

Britannica Kids: Kylian Mbappé
https://kids.britannica.com/students/article/Kylian-Mbappé/636145

Britannica Kids: World Cup
https://kids.britannica.com/students/article/World-Cup/487889

Greenberg, Keith Elliot: *France National Soccer Teams: Ultimate Fan Guide*. Lerner Publications, 2026.

Kiddle: Thierry Henry facts for kids
https://kids.kiddle.co/Thierry_Henry

Lilley, Matt. *The FIFA World Cup*: Apex Editions, 2023.

Moon, Derek. *Kylian Mbappé: Soccer Superstar*: Press Box Books, 2025.

INDEX

Arsenal, 4–5, 10, 14–15, 21, 25
AS Monaco FC, 8–13

El Clásico, 15–16

FC Barcelona, 15–17
Footballer of the Year, 20

Golden Boot, 21, 23

Manchester United, 4, 11
Messi, Lionel, 17–19

Paris Saint-Germain (PSG), 13, 16–19, 22–23
Player of the Year, 21, 23

Real Madrid, 11, 15–16, 25

UEFA Champions League, 17, 23

Wenger, Arsène, 10
World Cup, 5–6, 18–23

PHOTO ACKNOWLEDGMENTS

Image credits: Stuart MacFarlane/Arsenal FC/Getty Images, p. 4; Christian Liewib/Corbis/Getty Images, p. 5; Etsuo Hara/Getty Images, p. 6; Michael Regan - UEFA/UEFA/Getty Images, p. 7; PATRICK HERTZOG/AFP/Getty Images, p. 8; Mark Leech/Offside/Getty Images, p. 9; Ben Radford/Getty Images, p. 10; Stu Forster/Getty Images, p. 11; Jean Catuffe/Getty Images, p. 12; VALERY HACHE/AFP/Getty Images, p. 13; Stuart MacFarlane/Arsenal FC/Getty Images, p. 14; Etsuo Hara/Getty Images, p. 15; Denis Doyle/Getty Images, p. 16; Mustafa Yalcin/Anadolu Agency/Getty Images, p. 17; Andrew Surma/NurPhoto/Getty Images, p. 18; ODD ANDERSEN/AFP/Getty Images, p. 19; Clive Mason/Getty Images, p. 20; Stuart MacFarlane/Arsenal FC/Getty Images, p. 21; FRANCK FIFE/AFP/Getty Images, p. 22; Michael Regan - FIFA/FIFA/Getty Images, p. 23; Alex Caparros/Getty Images, p. 24; Phil Cole/Getty Images, p. 25; Jasper Juinen/Getty Images, p. 26; David Ramos/Getty Images, p. 27; Stuart MacFarlane/Arsenal FC/Getty Images, p. 28; Alexander Hassenstein/Getty Images, p. 29.

Cover: Guillermo Martinez/Sipa USA/Newscom; MYSTY/SIPA/Newscom.